RAINBOW PRAYERS

PRAYERS AND REFLECTIONS FOR A SUSTAINABLE WORLD

GAYNOR COBB

KEVIN MAYHEW LTD

First published in 2021 by Kevin Mayhew Ltd,
Rattlesden,
Stowmarket,
Suffolk, IP14 3BW
www.kevinmayhew.com

ISBN (paperback) 978-1-8385-8102-2
ISBN (eBook) 978-1-8385-8103-9
Paperback product code 1501682
eBook product code 1501683

Created with Vellum

To the Where Rainbows Meet community-based organisation in the Vrygrond Township in Cape Town, South Africa.

And to Owen James Emmanuel Maltby, born during Advent 2020, on 18th December.

CONTENTS

"Do your little bit of good where you are; it's those little bits of good put together that overwhelm the world."

(*Desmond Tutu*)

1

INTRODUCTION

The Bible is full of the colours of the Rainbow. God's promise to Noah was given in the form of a rainbow, making a covenant between God and man. People are still inspired by the hope a rainbow brings as beauty and calm after a storm. It suggests that we have overcome adversity and that there is hope for the future. Even though we understand how a rainbow occurs, it seems out of the ordinary, a connection to God.

At the Last Supper, Jesus told his disciples that the wine was the new covenant in his blood, poured out for them. Jesus, the Christ was God's promise. The Messiah, bringing his own message and way to God's kingdom.

This is a book of prayers, readings and reflections, using rainbow colours as a starting point. White is included for white light and silver as a raindrop glistening when a rainbow appears. Readings are taken from the Old and New Testament. Each colour chapter is divided into six sections. At the end of each chapter, I consider one or more of the seventeen United Nations Sustainable Development Goals with thought and prayer. These are aims for all nations and people of the world, including the eradication of poverty and inequality. They are linked with colour icons and I have used these colours as my connection to their themes.

I hope that both individuals and churches will remember the United Nations Sustainable Development Goals frequently in their intercessions. Perhaps their achievement is the gold at the end of the rainbow. It is certainly our hope for the future, our covenant with God and an aim that we as Christians should always hold in our prayers.

2

NOAH'S RAINBOW

> God said, 'This is the sign of the covenant that I make between me and you and every living creature that is with you, for all future generations: I have set my (rain)bow in the clouds, and it shall be a sign of the covenant between me and the earth."
>
> Genesis 9:12-13

reflection

God's rainbow was a sign of a new life for Noah and his family. It was a promise of a future filled with hope and God's promise that he would not send a flood again. Noah had made an altar to God and the scent of the offerings had been pleasing to the Lord. God made a covenant with Noah and his people going forward. There are two sides to this promise and humankind had to keep their own promise to the Almighty that they would worship only him and keep his laws.

Today when we see a rainbow, we smile and feel the same hope. There is something magical about the colours in the sky even though we know that it is the splitting of the white light through raindrops when the sun comes out behind the clouds.

During the worldwide pandemic in 2020, the rainbow appeared in windows everywhere to show hope once again and to demonstrate support to hospital workers.

It told us not to give up but to weather the storm so that one day we would see the rainbow just as Noah did and know that there would be a brighter future.

It is still the promise from God to have faith and know that difficulties can be overcome as long as we believe.

Prayer

Loving Lord,
We thank you for your promise of hope,
shown by the beautiful colours of the rainbow.
May we hold this in our hearts
whenever we feel the sadness
of difficulty
or despair.

Help us to see
that whenever our lives
fill with rain,
there is always a better tomorrow.

May we take this sign into the future,
as an opportunity given
to reach out to others.

Help us to take your covenant
to all people
so that they can make their commitment
to you.
And that by placing ourselves
in your loving hands
we may find the comfort
and certainty
of your healing love.

Amen.

RED

3

MAN FROM DUST

Then the Lord God formed man from the dust of the ground, and breathed into his nostrils the breath of life; and the man became a living being.

Genesis 2:7

reflection

The root word for mankind is 'oudem', which means red clay. Adam was formed from dust and so the colour red is linked with life itself, representing humanity.

Adam and Eve were tempted by Satan as the snake in the Garden of Eden. Eating from the tree of knowledge caused them to commit original sin.

Humankind is on a journey throughout the ages to return to God the Father and to be once more in a state of grace.

Throughout this time, people are learning life lessons. If we look at the words of Jesus, such as those of the parables and the Sermon on the Mount, we can find the way to restore ourselves to God's grace and prepare ourselves for eternal life.

Jesus Christ died for us on the cross for the forgiveness of sins, to bring us to the Father.

In this way, we are able to receive the absolution for the forgiveness of our sins when we truly repent. We make our journey following Jesus and through the power of the cross.

Prayer

Eternal Father,
We give you thanks
for all that we are.

Forgive us
that we turned from you
in our sinfulness.

Guide us
on our life journey
that we may find our way forward.

Help us
to understand the world around us
and our place within it.

May we know your will
and withstand temptation.
Lead us towards a life of service
which rejects selfish demands.

We pray,
that restored to your grace,
we may once again
know the completeness
of your love
through Jesus Christ,
our Saviour.

Amen.

4

PASSOVER

> They shall take some of the blood and put it on the two doorposts and the lintel of the houses in which they eat it.
>
> The blood shall be a sign for you on the houses where you live: when I see the blood, I will pass over you, and no plague shall destroy you when I strike the land of Israel.
>
> Exodus 12:7 and 13

reflection

In the Old Testament, blood of a slaughtered lamb was smeared onto the doorposts of the children of Israel, so that the Lord God could pass over them to save them from the plague that was to strike Egypt. This was the origin of the first Jewish Passover. The blood of the animal was a sign to show that those in the house were God's people who should be saved. The children of Israel were safe when the Egyptians suffered God's plague.

Passover is still celebrated and door posts have a mezuzah fixed to them containing the words of the Jewish prayer the Shema Yisrael which starts with, ' Hear, O Israel; the Lord is our God, the Lord alone.'

This was an instruction from God which could also be regarded as a covenant because Judaism keeps the Passover every year.

Jesus is the ' Lamb of God' taking away the sin of the world. In this way, we think of the blood of the First Passover giving protection. This is a new covenant from God through his Son.

Prayer

Almighty God,
we give thanks for your covenant
with the children of Israel.
Their faith in you
brought them out of slavery in Egypt
and into the promised land.

We know that if we have faith in you,
we can overcome all the difficulties
that life brings
before us.

May we always remember
to give thanks and praise
in celebration.

Today,
when so many distractions
lead us to turn from you,
we think back,
to remember your great power.

We praise you
and glory in your Holy Name.
Aleluia!

Amen.

5

THE BLOOD OF CHRIST

> Indeed, God did not send the Son into the world to condemn the world, but in order that the world might be saved through him. Those who believe in him are not condemned; but those who do not believe are condemned already, because they have not believed in the name of the only Son of God.
>
> John 3:17-18

reflection

Red is the blood of Christ shed for us. Christ is given as a sacrifice to save humanity from sin. Jesus has put humanity right with God by dying on the cross so that sins may be forgiven and we can be restored to God's grace.

We know that there is still sin in the world but the death of Christ has given humanity the ability to come before God. If we repent with all our heart, we may be absolved of our sins and forgiven by our Father in heaven. This is because of the power of the cross of Jesus. We receive absolution before we come to the communion table to share in fellowship with Christ as Jesus taught us.

Christians need to feel cleansed of sin before accepting the Eucharist.

The wine of communion as the blood of Christ shed for us reminds us of the great sacrifice of Jesus. It was a high price to pay and this gives us such a great responsibility as we follow him. Blood courses through our veins giving us life and Jesus is life-giving as our Saviour. His sacrifice for our sins ' like scarlet' is a powerful image in the Christian Church.

We have the opportunity to believe in Jesus and to follow him so that we can be granted the gift of eternal life.

Prayer

Heavenly Father,
We thank you for the sacrifice of your Son
whose life was given for us.
In following him,
we know that the road ahead is hard,
perhaps because we suffer the pain of others,
as he did,
as well as our own pain.

We give thanks
that we are able to come to you
repenting of our sins,
knowing that you are merciful

because of the sacrifice
of Our Saviour.

May we always show awareness
of those around us.

Help us to strive
to relieve suffering
and to reach out
with healing love
as he did.

Amen.

6

REMEMBRANCE

> He shall judge between the nations, and shall arbitrate for many peoples; they shall beat their swords into ploughshares, and their spears into pruning hooks; nation shall not lift up sword against nation, neither, shall they learn war any more.
>
> Isaiah 2:4 gives us hope.

reflection

In the 20th century, red became the colour of remembrance, in particular because of the red poppies growing wild around the landscape of the First World War.

The image of falling poppies stays with us as we pray and remember those who have died in the service of their country, not just in the two world wars, but in other conflicts. We lay wreaths of poppies at our war memorials.

The USSR presented a statue to the United Nations in

December 1959. It was based on this wonderful Bible verse from Isaiah. The hope is still that it should inspire all world leaders to think of peace before war and of feeding the people rather than sending them to fight.

Prayer

Almighty Father,
We pray for all those
who have lost their lives
in war.

We think of the wild red poppies
blowing in the wind,
fragile as we can be.

We pray for peace and understanding
between all nations,
so that all people will go forward together,
healing divisions,
and working for the common good.

We bless all peacemakers.
May their voices be heard
above the noise
of dissent and violence,
intolerance and prejudice.

When we seek to know each other better,
we share the humanity
that binds us in your love.

Guide us towards reconciliation
where there is conflict.
May all nations hold strong in the desire
for lasting peace.

We pray especially for the United Nations
as one voice of the people.
May we move towards the light of your love
in the true spirit of brotherhood.

Amen.

7

PENTECOST

> And suddenly from heaven there came a sound like the rush of a violent wind, and it filled the entire house where they were sitting. Divided tongues, as of fire, appeared among them, and a tongue rested on each of them. All of them were filled with the Holy Spirit and began to speak in other languages, as the Spirit gave them ability.
>
> Acts 2:2-4

reflection

Red is thought of as the colour of fire, even though it is not the only colour of a flame. It is the colour of the Holy Spirit and of Pentecost when the disciples received the power to continue Christ's work. It gave them the ability to understand and communicate in different languages and to spread the good news. Christians ask to be filled with the

Holy Spirit to do God's work when they reach out to others in his name and in the name of Christ. Many of us have felt the power of prayer, especially when together. Group prayer is taking place more often to bring strength and peace.

Prayer

Loving Father,
We thank you for the gift
of the Holy Spirit.
May we seek to know you better
and to do your will.
The Spirit is there if we truly desire it.

Help us to receive your Word
into our hearts,
to find within us,
the understanding and the power
of your Spirit.

When we struggle on life's path,
trying to show your love,
help us to look within
to find the spirit's inspiration.

Thus, calmed by your love,
and filled with your hope,
we may go forth into the world,
in your strength alone.

Amen.

8

KINGSHIP

> To him was given dominion and glory and kingship, that all peoples, nations and languages should serve him. His dominion is an everlasting dominion that shall not pass away, and his kingship is one that shall never be destroyed.
>
> Daniel 7:14

reflection

In the Old Testament, Daniel's dream predicted the coming of Christ as a king. Purple dye was expensive and so red also symbolised royalty. Today, it is the colour of martyrdom and sacrifice.

The sacrifice of Jesus Christ is uppermost in our minds as we think of red. His royalty also makes the connection between red and purple an understanding one.

Prayer

Eternal Father,
We come before you
in humility and awe,
glorying in your kingship.
You have given us the power of the cross
as a symbol of salvation and sacrifice.

We thank you for:
your cross of redemption;
your cross of hope;
your cross of faith;
your cross of salvation,
and your cross of healing love for humanity.

May the power of your Spirit
reach all the corners
of this damaged world
as we remember the sacrifice
of Our Lord and Saviour, Jesus Christ.

We ask for your blessing and guidance
as we travel the difficult road of salvation
bathed in his love and light.
May we hold high the triumphant cross
of hope and love for the world
given to us by Our Saviour.

Amen.

9

SUSTAINABLE DEVELOPMENT GOALS: RED

The United Nations Sustainable Goals use the colour red for the goals to focus on:

- Poverty
- Education
- Gender equality

These represent immense challenges to international progress. Education itself is an important way to eradicate poverty by providing opportunity through skills and knowledge.

Prayer

Heavenly Father,
we pray for the poor of the world,
for those for whom life is a daily struggle.
May richer nations be generous

with international aid
to help the disadvantaged.

We pray that all children
will have the opportunities
provided by education,
giving them a better future.
May all be treated with equality,
so that girls also have the advantage of
education and employment.

We know that the world is its people
and we must nurture them.
Father, help us to fight all inequalities
with the love that brings change.

Amen.

ORANGE/AMBER

10

THE GLORY OF GOD

> And there, the glory of the God of Israel was coming from the east; the sound was like the sound of mighty waters; and the earth shone with his glory.
>
> Ezekiel 43:2

reflection

Orange/Amber is similar to gold and is associated with majesty and the Glory of God.

Often, the Bible tells us about the grain which is so important for the survival of people, especially at times of famine, when the stores of grain prevent starvation. We remember this from the story of Joseph when he was able to store grain after his dream. This helped him to be of importance to Pharaoh.

Grain certainly can be regarded as having a golden value.

God's glory returned to the Temple, where grain had been offered.

It was a special offering in the Temple. The people shared the food that gave them life in the same way that they made sacrifices to God.

Prayer

Heavenly Father,
We give thanks for the harvest,
and for those who work hard
to provide our food.

You provide the sun and the rain,
nature with rich treasures,
your gifts to us.

The earth is indeed bright
with your glory!
Everything around us
shouts your name!
Each plant and leaf is different.
There are so many things to eat,
filling us with the goodness of life.

Help us not to take our food for granted,
but to save precious resources.

Amen.

11

FOOD IN THE WILDERNESS

> When the layer of dew lifted, there on the surface of the wilderness was a fine flaky substance, as fine as frost on the ground.
>
> Exodus 16:14

reflection

Orange is certainly the colour of harvest. The sheaf of corn standing at the front of the church as we give our thanks for God's gifts of food. At these times we often join together to break bread to celebrate everything we have and especially nature's bounty.

God sent food for the children of Israel so that they could survive in the wilderness. It was their harvest.

The food was a very fine covering on the ground. This was manna from heaven, feeding people where there was no likelihood that they would find anything. It rewarded them for the faith they showed in God on their journey to the promised land. I think David Kossoff described it as a bit like cornflakes. This was certainly a miracle.

Prayer

Loving Father,
we thank you for the earth's gifts of food.
For grain of every kind,
the bread of Heaven.

We pray for all those
who work on the land
and those who solve problems
such as irrigation.

The earth has so much food
and yet many still go hungry.
Help us to share
our wealth and resources.

As we reach out,
may all receive the food they need
flourishing in your harvest
of sustaining love.

Amen.

12

HARVEST

But as for what was sown on good soil, this is the one who hears the word and understands it, who indeed bears fruit and yields, in one case a hundredfold, in another sixty, and in another thirty.
Matthew 13: 23

reflection

We also think of ourselves as seed just as Jesus described in the parable of the sower.

The seed fell on the path, rocky ground with little soil, among thorns and also in good soil. Only the seed falling in good soil grew and brought forth grain, whereas the other seed either failed to grow or grew quickly but died or was choked.

We are the seed and in good soil we hear, understand and act on the word, without being drawn away by the temptations of the world around us or by difficult conditions.

Perhaps there are times we seem to be planted in good soil but other times we are not so sure.

Christians keep trying to find the good soil and to be the best grain that they can possibly be.

The sower asks why the crop failed and tries to sow in better conditions the following year.

Maybe as Christians we are hard on ourselves but we always keep trying and we are helped by prayer and the taking of communion.

Prayer

Lord Jesus,
thank you for the parables,
explaining your Word.
They show us the way to live our lives.

Help us to work hard
to be the seed in good soil,
even though we sometimes find ourselves
on stony ground.

May we listen to your word with our hearts
and read the Bible
with a mind open to your truth.

If we falter,
may we always be prepared to try again
aided in prayer by your guiding love.

Amen.

13

THE SABBATH

> One sabbath he was going through the cornfields; and as they made their way his disciples began to pluck heads of grain. The Pharisees said to him,'Look, why are they doing what is not lawful on the sabbath?' . . . Then he said to them, 'The sabbath was made for humankind, and not humankind for the sabbath; so the Son of Man is lord even of the sabbath.'
>
> Mark 2:23 -24 and 27-28

reflection

The sabbath day is a time to rest and worship God, but Jesus would not say that it was wrong to prepare food to eat. He was standing up to the Pharisees who wanted to keep to the very letter of the law.

Today, we find so many demands on our time and

Sunday is not as special and quiet as it once was. Being able to worship together is of great comfort and value to many Christians and the church family offers friendship, help and support one to another, just as a normal family does.

Prayer

Eternal Father,
thank you for Sunday,
when we can join with others to worship.
The power of prayer is greater
when we pray together
and the fellowship of one with another
helps us to understand
the Christian message of love for you
and love for our neighbour.

May we always value
this special time and place to seek you.
In the stillness of a quiet building,
in the joy of praise,
in the beauty of your word,
you are there.

Coming to the communion table
we are renewed
in the mystery of the sacrament.
May we be filled with the power of your Spirit
to go forth in your service.

Amen.

14

WORSHIP OF IDOLS

> The rest of humankind, who were not killed by these plagues, did not repent of the works of their hands or give up worshipping demons and idols of gold and silver and bronze and stone and wood, which cannot see or hear or walk.
>
> Revelation 9:20

reflection

The reading tells of the worship of idols which was forbidden by God.

Today, there are so many idols, including gold. Money, wealth, position, sex and power are worshipped in our consumer-led society. Yet, we are still amazed by friendship, love and charity. In the world pandemic which started in 2020, the rainbow signified caring support.

Communities reached out to help those in need. This

showed that humankind is capable of setting aside the idols and finding the love of God within themselves.

Prayer

Loving Father,
help us to see beyond
the clamour of our busy lives;
of commercialism, lights, social media
and twenty-four hour news.

Our needs and the idols of the modern age
are so many and they shout so loud.
May we rise above them to find
the stillness of silence.

Help us to notice the world around us.
In the wisdom of your word,
help us to cast out the demons of today.
Seeking you in prayer,
may we find the solace we need above all else.
In quiet contemplation let us seek calm.
Finding you, may we be guided
to do your will,
reaching out to others
in your name.

Amen.

15

LIVING STONES

> Come to him, a living stone, though rejected by mortals yet chosen and precious in God's sight, and like living stones, let yourselves be built into a spiritual house, to be a holy priesthood, to offer spiritual sacrifices acceptable to God through Jesus Christ.
>
> 1 Peter 2: 4-5

reflection

Palestinian Christians are known as 'Living Stones'. Some are families who are descended from the first Christians and there are only a small number of them. Only 2% of the population of Israel and the Palestinian territories were Christian in 2007.

The living stones are there, marking the places where the old stones of the Bible stories telling of the life of Jesus remain. Our Palestinian guide in the Holy Land said that he hoped that tourists would return home as pilgrims and pilgrims would leave the holy places as disciples.

In his first letter, Peter explained that ' living stones' were those rejected by man but chosen by God through Jesus Christ.

We may not be living stones but we can witness for Our Saviour, Jesus Christ.

There are many times today when we can stand as Christians in a world that forgets.

When we celebrate Christian festivals seen by the world as commercial opportunities, we can find the spiritual truth and significance. Somehow, I feel that it has become more important to show our Christianity than it once was. Perhaps I am saddened by the secular world, even though I understand that people should be free to worship or not to.

Prayer

Heavenly Father,

may we think of ourselves
as living stones.
Help us to stand up for Jesus
as today's disciples.

We pray for all the people of Palestine
and especially the Christian Palestinians
who remain as living stones
in the place where Jesus himself
walked the earth.

In so many ways
we are all pilgrims
on a journey,
seeking truth,
knowledge
and love.
May we share our faith and belief
with others,
giving of our certainty.
In the name of Jesus.

Amen.

16

SUSTAINABLE DEVELOPMENT GOALS: ORANGE/AMBER

The United Nations Sustainable Development Goals for orange/amber are to show a commitment to inclusivity through:

- Infrastructure, industry and innovation

With a focus on:

- Cities and the community

Working together we must strive to build villages, towns and cities to support people within communities, planning lives at the same time as buildings. We need to consider how people learn, work, enjoy family time and leisure, so that we can build for the future. As Christians, we must consider our local communities and beyond as we live in the global village of the world.

Prayer

Loving Father,
we pray for all who plan villages,
towns and cities.

May they work to bring
people together,
providing opportunities
for caring support,
especially for those
who are vulnerable and weak.

Help them to care for family life,
giving time to build
relationships.

We pray for creativity
and inclusive design,
healing divisions
as all people are valued
within real community life.

Amen.

YELLOW

17

WORSHIP

So they came, both men and women: all who were of a willing heart brought brooches and earrings and signet rings and pendants, all sorts of gold objects, everyone bringing an offering of gold to the Lord. Exodus 35:22

reflection

When Moses did not return from the mountain, the people asked his brother Aaron, to make gods for them to worship. Aaron told the people to bring him their gold rings and he cast an image of a calf from a mould. The people worshipped the idol and God was angry.

Some time later, after God had given Moses new tablets of stone upon which the commandments were written, the people prepared a tabernacle for the Lord.

This was not an idol to be worshipped, but a portable

place of worship where they could concentrate their devotion to the Lord even while they were on a journey to the promised land. In this way, they would be reminded that the lord God was holy and to be worshipped.

Prayer

Eternal Father,
help us to know all that glitters
is not gold.

May we seek the gold
that comes from your word.

Guide us to know you better
and to do your will.

May we turn away from the temptations
and idols worshipped in the secular world.

So many things can be used for good,
helping others in your name.

When we worship,
may we come to you
in humble faith.

Amen.

18

THE SUN

> And when you look up to the heavens and see the sun, the moon, and the stars, all the host of heaven, do not be led astray and bow down to them and serve them, things that the Lord your God has allotted to all the peoples everywhere under heaven.
>
> Deuteronomy 4:19

reflection

God made it clear to the Israelites that they should not worship idols in a human or animal form. He also told them not to worship the sun, moon or stars. These he said, are given to everyone.

It would have been easy for people to worship the sun that gave light and warmth or the moon and stars lighting the dark night sky, but knowing that they came from God and that he had made it clear to them how he wished to be worshipped gave them a special covenant with the Lord.

Prayer

Eternal Father,
we thank you
for the sun giving warmth and light:
our crops grow
and our countryside is full of life.

We know
that everything in creation
comes from you.

We marvel
at the sun and planets in space
and the beauty of all things
on the earth.

May we always appreciate
this great gift
celebrating the riches
of life
around us.

Amen.

19

SEASONS

If you will only heed his every commandment that I am commanding you today-loving the Lord your God, and serving him with all your heart and with all your soul-then he will give the rain for your land in its season, the early rain and the later rain, and you will gather in your grain, your wine, and your oil.' Deuteronomy 11:13-14

reflection

This is the first of the great commandments that Jesus gave when he was asked by the Pharisee lawyer for the greatest commandment, to love God with all your heart and soul. As a reward for serving God, the rain provided the harvest and there was a time of plenty.

We celebrate God's creation and especially the harvest of food each year. The seasons have their own influence in nature. In this way we celebrate God's gifts to us, knowing they are gifts in themselves. The beautiful colours of Autumn delight our senses and when we crunch golden leaves underfoot, we know that the trees lying dormant for the winter season will be green again in the spring after their rest. One season helps to prepare for another and we give thanks to God all year round.

Prayer

Heavenly Father,
we thank you for the seasons,
As each brings its own blessings.

We bring our worship
before you,
humbled by the beauty
around us.

The snow of winter
throws a magical blanket of captivation.

In spring,
shoots of new life promise hope.

Fields of corn
shining in the early morning sunshine
gladden our hearts
in summer.

And autumn days glow

with trees of many colours.

Creation shouts your name
when golden light shimmers
on the sea.

Even as light fades,
the sky deepens red gold.

All people must praise you
for this earth.
Your glory is everywhere!

Amen.

20

STORING WEALTH

> By your wisdom and your understanding you have amassed wealth for yourself, and have gathered gold and silver into your treasuries. By your great wisdom in trade you have increased your wealth, and your heart has become proud in your wealth.
>
> Ezekiel 28:4-5

reflection

These verses speak of the storing of wealth in a selfish way, as Ezekiel challenges the King of Tyre with God's message.

Self-centred wealth creation without thought for others, and the corruption often found when those in governments take money for themselves, rather than for the people they serve, is still a problem today.

We know that at the moment, the planet has the

resources to look after everyone but we are a long way from achieving equal access to food, water and other basic necessities.

The pandemic which started in 2020 has accentuated inequalities all over the world, especially where people were reliant on casual work. Providing food for those who would have otherwise gone hungry was important and many organisations prepared and delivered supplies to those in need.

Prayer

Loving Father,
please forgive us
when we fail you.
May we cast out all
selfish thoughts.

Guide us when we are preoccupied
by our own concerns,
unable to see
that the needs of others around us
are greater.

Make us aware
of the world and its problems,
so that we can give aid
to those in difficulty.

We give thanks for all charities,
for money raised,
and for the work they do.

We pray that nations govern wisely,
aiding the weak
within societies.

May all seek to drive out hunger,
pain and fear.

Amen.

21

TRANSFIGURATION

> And he was transfigured before them, and his face shone like the sun, and his clothes became dazzling white. Suddenly there appeared to them Moses and Elijah, talking with him.
>
> Matthew 17:2-3

reflection

In Matthew 17, the Bible tells us about the Transfiguration, when Jesus went up a high mountain with Peter, James and John. His appearance changed even as they looked upon him and he was seen to be talking with Moses and Elijah.

The face of Jesus was shining like the sun, showing a holy radiance of being. The light shone from his face and his clothes dazzled. This was during the ministry of Jesus, before he went into Jerusalem. It was an indication of what was to come but he asked the disciples not to tell anyone about it until after he had been raised from the dead. He told them that he was going to suffer death and this must have been so difficult for them to understand and to accept in their hearts and minds.

Prayer

Eternal Father,
there are so many things
we do not understand
while we are here
on the earth.

We give thanks
for the life and ministry of Jesus,
and of his disciples,
who looked on in wonder
at the Transfiguration,
as we would have done.

Lord Jesus showed us heavenly light,
when he became a dazzling, radiant being.
May we seek to accept the mysteries
of life eternal,
even though they are beyond
our earthly understanding.
And through Your Holy Spirit,
may we seek to show your love.

Amen.

22

FAITH

> So that the genuineness of your faith-being more precious than gold that, though perishable, is tested by fire-may be found to result in praise and glory and honour when Jesus Christ is revealed. Although you have not seen him, you love him; and even though you do not see him now, you believe in him and rejoice with an indescribable and glorious joy, for you are receiving the outcome of your faith, the salvation of your souls.
>
> 1 Peter 1:7-9

reflection

In his first letter to the Christian exiles in five churches, Peter writes of the living hope of faith in Jesus.

Christians know that it is their faith in God and in Jesus Christ the Saviour that guides their lives. They hold Christ as the gold standard, asking ' what would Jesus do?' to questions and life decisions. It is the love of Jesus that drives them forward, certain in the knowledge that they are saved because of his resurrection. The name of Jesus means God Saves.

Prayer

Heavenly Father,
we give you thanks
for the gift of your Son,
Our Saviour, Jesus Christ.

As our faith in him grows,
our lives blossom
in love and service
to others.

Our purpose is strong
in the power
of the Spirit.

We dedicate ourselves
as disciples,
going forward
with Christ.

We follow where he leads,
even when the world around us
is fraught
with doubts.

We pray for strength
to carry his message
of hope and love,
holding high
the cross of salvation.

May our faith shine
with a brighter light,
a knowing,
soul-deep.

Amen.

23

SUSTAINABLE DEVELOPMENT GOALS: YELLOW/GOLD

The United Nations Sustainable Development Goals for yellow/gold are to:

- Achieve zero hunger
- Provide sufficient energy for all purposes

As we consider global warming, we need to change the way we produce and consume energy. Renewable energy sources, such as solar power and wind power are increasing in use as the planet faces greater challenges in feeding a growing population.

Prayer

Almighty God,
we pray for the poor of the world,
For those who lack food because of drought,
war or economic difficulty.

We pray for improved support
from richer to poorer nations,
and for fair distribution
within countries themselves.

May the nations of the world
join together
to solve the problems
of energy resources.

We pray for the desire
to produce renewable energy
and for truth and clarity
among energy producers.

May all people save energy resources
in order to help each other
and to protect
the environment.

Amen.

GREEN

24

GREEN PASTURES

> The Lord is my shepherd, I shall not want. He makes me lie down in green pastures; he leads me beside still waters; he restores my soul. He leads me in right paths for his name's sake.
>
> Psalm 23

reflection

This is a beautiful image of the good shepherd walking with us beside a river, where we find a comforting place to rest. When we lie down in green fields, staring up at a blue sky, we are soothed. Our troubled souls are restored by the tranquil water of the river running by.

We are led along the right paths to tread in life by the Saviour because this is the time he finds out about our difficulties. The psalm is a great comfort at times of trouble as it talks about God's support against evil.

Prayer

Heavenly Father,
we thank you
for the countryside,
for the green fields,
and for views that stretch miles ahead,
stirring and uplifting us.

The quiet of the countryside
stills our minds.
It is our medicine,
giving us good health.

At times of difficulty,
we can turn to you.
We are your sheep
and we seek
the good shepherd.

Everything around us
is formed by you
to perfection.

We praise your Holy name
in wonder.

Help us to preserve
green spaces and countryside
to benefit all people.

May we set aside paths
for safe walking
and also support those
who tend the land
to produce our food.

Help us
to exist together
in thoughtful cooperation.

Amen.

25

TREE BY THE WATERS

Blessed are those who trust in the Lord, whose trust is the Lord. They shall be like a tree planted by water, sending out its roots by the stream. It shall not fear when heat comes,

and its leaves shall stay green; in the year of drought it is not anxious, and it does not cease to bear fruit.

Jeremiah 17: 7-8

reflection

When we trust in the strength of God, we know that as Jesus said in Matthew 19, that all things are possible. The tree described above does not worry about drought because it has a water source with its roots by the stream.

God can manage our lives and help if we come to him in

prayer, because he understands us and knows the needs that we have. We can trust in his strength because with him everything is possible.

Trees have a special place in our hearts. They do represent strength. The English oak is a strong symbol of steadfastness and the olive tree is a symbol of the Mediterranean and of the Holy Land. The olive trees at Gethsemane are among the oldest in the world, even though it is not clear if they are linked in some way to those in the time of Christ. They give us the impression of ages past showing that we link ourselves to them because they reach deep into the earth and up into the sky.

Prayer

Heavenly Father,
we trust in your strength.

We are like trees,
with our roots near water,
growing and flourishing
because our needs are met.

The words of Jesus
give us food
for our hearts and minds.

We are fed
and gain eternal life
in him.

May we always heed your Word
and seek to understand
your divine truth.

In the name of the Father,
the Son,
and the Holy Spirit.

Amen.

26

THE FIG TREE

From the fig tree learn its lesson: as soon as its branch becomes tender and puts forth its leaves, you know that summer is near.

Matthew 24: 32-33

reflection

Jesus is speaking about reading signs. The fig tree gives a sign of new growth in summer. These signs are to be watched carefully because they tell us about God's kingdom. Jesus says that even after heaven and earth have ceased to exist, his words will remain.

This could suggest that there is a future beyond everything we know and think about. Words of Christ will be the most important guidance for humanity and all that survives. Jesus is speaking of eternal life.

The parable of the fig tree can also be compared to the

account of Jesus and the fig tree with no fruit. (Matthew 21:18-22) Although Jesus gives its withering as a response to faithful prayer, we wonder why he destroyed it. It can be seen as people who bear no fruit because they have not listened to the words of God and of the Son. In the Sermon on the Mount, Jesus talks of good fruit and bad fruit when he speaks of false prophets.

Prayer

Heavenly Father,
help us to listen
to your Word,
and to bear fruit
like the fertile fig tree.

May our prayers
produce the good fruit
of positive action
to serve others.

We pray for all who have lost their way.
May they receive the water of life
from the Saviour,
that they too may be restored to your grace
and flourish like a beautiful fig tree
in summer.

Amen.

27

THE FEEDING OF THE FIVE THOUSAND

> Taking the five loaves and the two fish, he looked up to heaven, and blessed and broke the loaves, and gave them to his disciples to set before the people; and he divided the two fish among them all. And all ate and were filled; and they took up twelve baskets full of broken pieces and of the fish.
>
> Mark 6:41-43

reflection

This is a miracle of Jesus, which reminds us of the wine at the wedding in Cana. We can see that Christ is more than special. His divinity is clearly felt. The disciples in particular knew how little food there was and how far it went.

Jesus spent much of his time talking to the people. Mark 6 tells us of the occasion when people had followed the Lord and gathered on the green grass to listen to him. It became late and they had not eaten. They had five loaves and two fish, certainly not enough to go round the great crowd.

The miracle can also be viewed in another way. Even a few words of Jesus feed us with the divine and yet we can't hear enough, we hunger for more. Once again, we think about the importance of the words of Jesus. There is also the feeling that time stands still when listening to Jesus and there is no thought of the ordinary needs of living, such as food

Prayer

Heavenly Father,
we pray for the well being
of the people of the world,
especially after the suffering
of a pandemic.

We have been reminded
of the need to care
for each other
and to think about the consequences
of our own actions.

Be with all those
who feel lonely
or isolated.

May the bereaved feel your loving support,
cherishing fond memories,
as they face each new day.

Help us all to work towards
a positive future,
filled with the love and hope
of Our Saviour
Jesus Christ.

We ask this,
in his name.

Amen.

28

THE TRUE VINE

I am the true vine, and my Father is the vine-grower. He removes every branch in me that bears no fruit. Every branch that bears fruit he prunes to make it bear more fruit. You have already been cleansed by the word that I have spoken to you.

John 15: 1-3

reflection

The message of listening and heeding the word continues in the Gospel of St. John, when Jesus talks of being the true vine. Jesus is the vine grown by God and tended carefully to bear fruit. The disciples will be the fruit of the vine, giving the word of Jesus to the people when Jesus has returned to the Father. This brings us to the fellowship where we receive the blood of Christ through the wine of the sacrament.

Jesus tells his disciples to love one another as he has loved them, according to his own commandment. He is speaking of the way in which the disciples have followed his word and of the joy that will be complete because of his love. He is telling them that they will know how to reach out to each other and to strangers because they are bearing the fruit of the true vine and that is himself. They will be able to do God's work in the world.

Prayer

Heavenly Father,
help us to know you as the vine grower
and Lord Jesus as the true vine.

When we drink the wine of life
made from your Word,
help us to tend our hearts with your love
so we bear the best fruit.

May we be disciples,
bringing the good news
to those who have not heard your call.

Our joy will be found
through your life and love.
We pray that strangers will become
our brothers and sisters in Christ,
filled with your calming peace.

Amen.

29

RESURRECTION

Jesus said to her, ' Woman, why are you weeping? For whom are you looking? Supposing him to be the gardener, she said to him, ' Sir, if you have carried him away, tell me where you have laid him, and I will take him away.' Jesus said to her, ' Mary!' She turned and said to him in Hebrew, ' Rabbouni! (which means Teacher). Jesus said to her,' Do not hold on to me, because I have not yet ascended to the Father. But go to my brothers and say to them, ' I am ascending to my Father and your Father, to my God and your God.' John 20:15-17.

reflection

Jesus appeared to Mary Magdalene who had come to the tomb early on Sunday morning with other women to anoint the body. It may be significant that he appeared to a woman, because women were not regarded as reliable witnesses. Mary Magdalene was known to him as a female disciple and was there at the crucifixion. We associate Easter and the resurrection with the new life of spring and green shoots.

Jesus gives us a renewed sense of purpose and hope. He has defeated death itself and so we know that if we believe in him we will be granted eternal life. It is the empty cross symbolising victory that shows the power of Christ. It is a wonderful sign of strength and hope, empowering us and sustaining us in prayer. Holding crosses are used as an aid to prayer, giving comfort and support.

Prayer

Loving Father,
Jesus Christ is risen, Alleluia!

We give thanks for the life of Jesus,
God among us,
walking the earth as we do.

His victory over death
gives us hope.
The empty cross
is flooded with light
because we know that our saviour lives.
This is our celebration.

Help us on our own journey of life.
May we carry the power of the cross
into the hearts of all people,
showing love
and an ever stronger and deeper faith.

As the joy of the Easter message is felt
in all the corners of the earth,
we praise Father, Son and Holy Spirit.

The Lord is risen.
He is risen indeed!

Alleluia!

30

SUSTAINABLE DEVELOPMENT GOALS: GREEN

The United Nations Sustainable Development Goals for green are:

- Health and well-being
- Climate
- Action on Land

Worldwide health and well being depends on climate in many ways because drought and the famine this causes has such an impact on the people of poorer nations. War and situations of conflict also disrupt farming and settlements. This relates to the land itself and there are a number of initiatives to help states with resources and development.

As the world moves forward with plans to combat climate change, positive steps can be taken to help progress. Renewable energy, recycling and reusing are some of the ways that countries are moving forward in a positive way to make a difference.

Prayer

Almighty God,
we know that our planet is suffering
because we have used resources
without considering the future.

Help us to think about our actions
and listen to sensible advice.

May we seek new ways to live
in order to protect our environment.

Help us to reuse and recycle
our everyday needs
and also save water and energy,
so that all may share in a positive future.

May we preserve green land
with grass and trees,
so that we help to stop global warming.

We pray that all people
will love and care
for our beautiful earth.

Amen.

BLUE

31

SEA AND SKY

> And God said, ' Let there be a dome in the midst of the waters, and let it separate the waters from the waters.' So God made the dome and separated the waters that were under the dome from the waters that were above the dome. And it was so. God called the dome Sky. And there was evening and there was morning, the second day.
>
> Genesis 1:6

reflection

In creation, God separated the waters of the earth from the sky, which was like a dome over the water. The earth as a blue planet of beauty shows a spirit of uplift, when the bright blue of the sky is reflected in the water. The blue of water is calming and the depths suggest the mysteries of the soul.

Prayer

Eternal Father,
we give thanks
for the beauty of the sea,
reflecting the sky
on a bright day.

Our spirits
are uplifted!

As with a rainbow
after the storm,
the blue sky
breaking through the clouds
brings a positive mood,
even if we have felt weighed down
by the cares
of the world.

Help us
to find our own
blue sky!

May we find the right words
to lift the spirits
of those around us.
Amen.

32

PAVEMENT OF SAPPHIRE

Then Moses and Aaron, Nadab, and Abihu, and seventy of the elders of Israel went up, and they saw the God of Israel. Under his feet there was something like a pavement of sapphire stone, like the very heaven for clearness. God did not lay his hand on the chief men of the people of Israel; also they beheld God, and they ate and drank.

Exodus 24: 9-11.

reflection

Moses and a group of the Elders of Israel went to see God. The Bible tells of them going up to the mountain, where they were closer to God. In the same way, Jesus often went up a mountain to speak with the Father.

The blue of the sapphire pavement shows the majesty of God and echoes the blue planet of sky and sea. It is as though God himself loves the colour blue especially. We imagine something magnificent and sparkling, clear as heaven itself.

Precious gemstones are often used in the Bible to show opulence and here we have something truly amazing. One sapphire itself would be beautiful, but a whole pavement under God's feet shows something we would not find anywhere on earth itself, even in the richest palace. This would be so magnificent that those present would never forget the experience.

Prayer

Almighty Father,
we praise your holy name.
We come before you
in awe.

The beauty of sparkling sapphire
helps us to imagine Heaven.
Everywhere,
we see the wonder of your creation.
The sparkling sea
and bright blue of the sky
reflect your glory.

They declare your majesty: Alleluia!
May we be worthy
of all that you provide.

Each flower is like a jewel
in our earthly paradise.
May we care for our beautiful world,
tending it in your name.

Amen.

33

WATER FROM THE WELL

Jesus answered her, ' If you knew the gift of God, and who it is that is saying to you, 'Give me a drink', you would have asked him, and he would have given you living water.'(John 4:10) Jesus said to her, ' Everyone who drinks of this water will be thirsty again, but those who drink of the water that I will give them will never be thirsty. The water that I will give will become in them a spring of water gushing up to eternal life.' John 4: 13-14

reflection

This is one of the most important references to water for Christians. The Samaritan woman was surprised that Jesus asked her for a drink of water because Jews and Samaritans would not share anything.

We talk of the thirst for knowledge and yet the thirst for

the life of the Holy Spirit within, through knowledge of and worship of Jesus Christ gives eternal life itself.

Jesus is saying that this is possible and the woman was a person that he would not be expected to reach out to. Once again, Jesus is there for sinners and people who are not regarded as respectable. Jesus knew about the woman's life and she knew that a Messiah was coming.

The Gospel of John is the more spiritual of the Gospels and so it is not surprising that Jesus discusses the water of eternal life and also the worship of God in spirit and truth. We must seek to connect with God who is spirit and this is the only way to reach him.

Prayer

Heavenly Father,
thank you for sending your son, Jesus Christ,
to guide us to you.

May we seek to know you more clearly
through the power
of the Holy Spirit.

Welcoming Jesus
as the living water
is a life- changing experience.

We pray that we may thirst
for the opportunity to worship you
in spirit and in truth.

Help us to be mindful of this,
especially as we approach
the communion table.

May we always recognise
that through you,
we receive food and water
for our souls.

Amen.

34

SEA OF GALILEE

As he walked by the Sea of Galilee, he saw two brothers, Simon, who is called Peter, and Andrew his brother, casting a net into the lake-for they were fishermen. And he said to them, ' Follow me, and I will make you fish for people.' Immediately they left their nets and followed him.

Matthew 4: 18-20

reflection

In the New Testament we think of Galilee as a positive, productive time in the ministry of Jesus. The blue of the Sea of Galilee and the more peaceful surroundings suggest a time of calm before the storm of the tragic events of Jerusalem. It is still the same today, with a restful atmosphere and a surprising amount of green around the blue sea.

The Galilean fishermen left everything they knew and

placed their trust in Jesus. In the ministry around Capernaum, we find the blue of Galilee in our minds. The storm on the Sea of Galilee was stilled by Jesus when he was in a boat with his disciples. He awoke from sleep to find the boat swamped with the waves. He questioned the disciples' lack of faith but when he rebuked the winds and the sea, all was calm. This was another example of the power that Jesus had over the elements.

The storm also represents the trials of life. When we place our faith in the Father, Son and Holy Spirit, we can overcome all troubles. It can seem as though we are tossed about on a sea of worries. Jesus brings a calming of the storms of our minds.

Prayer

Almighty Father,
we thank you for the blue of sea and sky,
for bright optimism
and cheerfulness.

When trouble comes,
may we hold faith
in our hearts.

Jesus calmed the storm on Galilee,
showing his disciples
that with faith,
our worries
become small.

It is difficult at times,
yet Jesus is there,
giving peace.

May we always come to you
in prayer,
bringing our fears
for those we love,
bringing ourselves.

Amen.

35

JESUS WALKS ON WATER

And early in the morning he came walking towards them on the lake. But when the disciples saw him walking on the lake, they were terrified, saying, 'It is a ghost!' And they cried out in fear. But immediately Jesus spoke to them and said,'Take heart, it is I; do not be afraid.' Peter answered him, ' Lord, if it is you, command me to come to you on the water.' He said, 'Come.' So Peter got out of the boat, started walking on the water, and came towards Jesus. But when he noticed the strong wind, he became frightened, and beginning to sink, he cried out,' Lord save me!' Jesus immediately reached out his hand and caught him, saying to him,'You of little faith, why did you doubt?' Matthew 14: 25-32

reflection

Another demonstration of faith was also associated with water. Once again the Sea of Galilee was stormy and the disciples were in a boat. Peter's absolute trust faltered and that was enough to make him start to slip into the water.

Peter often seems to be like us. He wants to do the right thing and he does have confidence in the power of Jesus, but somehow it goes wrong. He is desperate to show his faith and it almost goes perfectly but not quite. He is helping us to learn a lesson. When we doubt ourselves, we need to dig deeper into our faith but our human frailty is so near the surface. Sometimes we think too much and we wonder what others will think of us.

Prayer

Almighty Father,
we ask you to be with us
when we suffer doubts.

We know that our faith wavers,
as Peter's did,
when he walked
on the water.

Help us to be strong
in our faith in you
and in our saviour,
Jesus Christ.

With the knowing within,
that you are always holding us
in your hands,
may we go forward with confidence.

Help us to put unworthy thoughts aside.
As Christians, trusting in your love,
may we bring hope
to the world.

Amen.

36

JESUS WASHES HIS DISCIPLES' FEET

> After he had washed their feet, had put on his robe, and had returned to the table, he said to them, ' Do you know what I have done to you? You call me Teacher and Lord – and you are right, for that is what I am. So if I, your Lord and Teacher have washed your feet, you also ought to wash one another's feet. For I have set you an example, that you also should do as I have done to you.'
>
> John 13:12- 15

Reflection

Peter was embarrassed when Jesus washed his feet. Once again, he was quick to make a judgement as we often are and he expressed the feelings that we would have had if Jesus had washed our feet. Jesus was showing his disciples that they must serve others as he had served them, even though he was the Master Jesus.

Washing the dust from feet when going inside a building was important in Jesus's time and the idea of purification in order to be able to take part in ritual or worship was significant.

It was the act of a servant and of course we know Jesus as the Servant King. Jesus was giving an important message to his followers that they should serve others, reaching out in his name.

The Holy Spirit was to fill the disciples but Jesus gave them an instruction to be humble and also to love and care for each other as he had loved and cared for them. This was especially clear because it was carried out at the last supper they enjoyed together before his arrest, trial and death.

Prayer

Heavenly Father,
fill our hearts with the humble service
shown by Jesus
as he washed the feet of his followers
at the Last Supper.

As Christians,
we think of ourselves as disciples.
May we serve others
as Jesus wished.

There are so many needs around us
and also in distant places.
Help us to make a difference in the world.

Sometimes even the smallest challenge
can seem too much
for us to bear.

Yet, with your help,
may we rise above our own shortcomings
to help others.

Trusting in your love
and filled with the power of your Spirit,
may we tread the path of service
to make a difference.

Amen.

37

SUSTAINABLE DEVELOPMENT GOALS: BLUE

The United Nations Sustainable Development Goals for Blue are:

- Clean Water
- Sanitation
- Life Below Water

These goals are vital for all communities and there are many projects all over the world where improvements are being made, including repairs to broken boreholes and infrastructure.

By 2050, at least one in four people is likely to live in a country affected by chronic or recurring shortages of fresh water.

Looking after our seas and oceans, preserves marine life which is also an important part of God's creation. Life below water ensures that we reduce pollution and overfishing to protect the blue planet.

Prayer

Heavenly Father,
we give thanks for water,
quenching our thirst,
washing clothes, washing people.

For the rain,
growing crops for food
and cleansing our world.

We know that many people
do not have access to clean water
and that this is a growing problem.

We pray for all those
working to help with irrigation,
improve water supplies,
and provide efficient sanitation.

Help us to raise awareness of hygiene,
and also conservation,
to prevent disease.

We pray for the success of all projects
providing help where there is need.

May governments support and work
for improvements for all people.

Amen.

INDIGO

38

LIGHT AND THE NIGHT SKY

> And God said, ' Let there be lights in the dome of the sky to separate the day from the night; and let them be for signs and for seasons and for days and years, and let them be lights in the dome of the sky to give light upon the earth.'
>
> Genesis.1:14

reflection

When God created the world, he created light. When we think of creation, we think of science and yet when we think of how, we do not always think of why.

When we see the wonders of God's creation, many of us still wonder about the great power behind such an amazing mystery. Even where science explains convincingly how things happen, they can seem quite random in occurrence and this does not sit easily with Christian belief.

Prayer

Heavenly Father,
forgive us when we do not understand
the mysteries of your universe.
Open our minds
to the surprising world we live in
and to all possibilities.

You separated light
from darkness
and made mankind
custodians of your creation.

So many times man has brought darkness
to your world,
in words and deeds,
many committed in your holy name.

Give strength
to all those who fight against evil
and against ignorance.

We thank you for heavenly light
and for Jesus Christ
who is the light of the world.
May your light shine in all dark places
and bring light into the hearts of all people.

Amen.

39

SPECIAL CLOTHES

> The Lord said to Moses: Speak to the Israelites, and tell them to make fringes on the corners of their garments throughout their generations and to put a blue cord on the fringe at each corner. You have the fringe so that, when you see it, you will remember all the commandments of the Lord and do them, and not follow the lust of your own heart and your own eyes. So you shall remember and do all my commandments, and you shall be holy to your God.
>
> Numbers 15: 37-40

reflection

God instructed Moses to tell the Israelites to wear special clothes to remind them of the commandments. The Israelites were instructed to use blue cord in particular. God had led them out of Egypt and this was one of the ways that they would be able to remember their covenant with him.

We do not have anything to help us to remember how to keep God's commandments or to guide our behaviour. When he was asked by a scribe which commandment was the greatest of all, Jesus spoke of two commandments which he called the greatest commandments.

Jesus referred to The Shema, from the Torah, which begins, Hear O Israel, the Lord our God is one. Jesus is reminding us of the most important promises we can make and it is around these commandments that Christianity is founded. If we know nothing else, we will understand how we should be Christian. There is a simplicity here but it is so important and if the world held these truths above all, surely it would be beautiful indeed.

Prayer

Lord Jesus,
help us to keep
your greatest commandments,
to love God
and to love others.

When we follow your Word,
we feel that we are Christians,
even though it is often hard to live
to your highest standards.

We do not have special clothes,
but we have the power of the cross

to remind us
of your love
and sacrifice.

We give thanks
for your supporting love,
as we walk with you
through life.

Amen.

40

GOD IS OUR REFUGE AND STRENGTH

> God is our refuge and strength, a very present help in trouble. Therefore we will not fear, though the earth should change, though the mountains shake in the heart of the sea . . . 'Be still, and know that I am God! I am exalted among the nations, I am exalted in the earth.'
>
> Psalm 46:1-3, 10

reflection

The psalm tells us of the strength of God and the threat of natural disasters. Once again, it is faith in God as a refuge when disaster strikes that is important. Our faith gives a stillness that provides quiet confidence whatever happens to us.

We can feel blown in every direction but if we put our

faith in God all will be well. In some ways this is a child-like faith and yet it is like a child that we enter heaven.

Jesus said 'Truly I tell you, unless you change and become like children, you will never enter the kingdom of Heaven.' The great words of the psalm, 'Be still and know that I am God,' tell us to seek God in the silence, to take time away from the noise of our daily lives to find him.

Prayer

Loving Father,
You are indeed our refuge and strength.
Help us to trust in you
as a child trusts in a parent.

When the storm rages,
you give us calm.

May we be always humble,
knowing that we do not understand,
but seek to learn your will.

May we seek you in the silence,
finding quiet times
away from the noise and demands
of modern life.

We know that if we come to you in prayer
we will find you.

Amen.

41

WALKING IN THE LIGHT OF GOD

The First Letter of John tells us that God is Light. This is the message we have heard from him and proclaim to you, that God is light and in him there is no darkness at all. If we say that we have fellowship with him while we are walking in darkness, we lie and do not do what is true; but if we walk in the light as he himself is in the light, we have fellowship with one another, and the blood of Jesus his Son cleanses us from all sin.

1 John 1: 5-7

reflection

We must seek to walk in the light of God in all that we do and uphold the truth at all times. We cannot be with him if we lie because we would be in the darkness.

God took the darkness of sin and created the light of love

through his Son, our Saviour Jesus Christ. When we confess our sins we can be cleansed because Jesus died for us but this does not mean that we walk in the darkness of sin. We must try to live in the light of God in all we do. This is our fellowship loving one another as Jesus taught his disciples (John 15:12).

Prayer

Almighty Father,
help us to walk
in the light of your love.

May we turn away from the darkness
of lies and sin.

We know that we will only find you
in the light,
and that the truth will lead us
in the way of righteousness.

May we share the light of love
with all people.

Let us bring the light of your healing
into every dark place.

Amen.

42

FAITH, NOT THE WISDOM, OF MEN

When I came to you, brothers and sisters, I did not come proclaiming the mystery of God to you in lofty words or wisdom. For I decided to know nothing among you except Jesus Christ, and him crucified. And I came to you in weakness and in fear and in much trembling. My speech and my proclamation were not with plausible words of wisdom, but with a demonstration of the Spirit and of power, so that your faith might rest not on human wisdom but on the power of God.

1 Corinthians 2:1-5

reflection

As mankind relies more and more upon the power of science to explain and guide the world, faith in God has declined. The idols of money, and power have been joined by science, so that attempts have even been made to cheat death with science such as cryogenics, where bodies are frozen in the hope that they can be revived at a later date. The normal rhythm of life and death would be interrupted.

Prayer

Eternal father,
in your power, in your son,
May we always seek you.

We thank you for knowledge,
for science with the ability
to help the world.

Even though we can solve many problems,
may we always seek you.

Eternal mysteries
are still far off.
We do not understand
the greatest questions of purpose.
We place our trust
in your love.

Amen.

43

LOVE, NOT FEAR

> For this reason I remind you to rekindle the gift of God that is within you through the laying on of my hands. For God did not give us a spirit of cowardice, but rather a spirit of power and of love and of self-discipline.
>
> 2 Timothy 1: 6-7

reflection

The gift of God is the courage to be our best selves and to reach out with love. It is to walk in the light of God. Christ with life eternal dwells within us, so that we are able to serve God in the power of the Holy Spirit. We are the 'living sacrifice' that Christ himself was when he died for us. We must go where Jesus leads and the path is not easy. His healing love can help us along the difficult road.

GAYNOR COBB

Prayer

Heavenly father,
we thank you for your gift of love,
and of your Holy Spirit,
helping us in all we do in your name.

We give thanks for your special gift,
the greatest of all,
that of your son,
who walked the earth

May we strive to live as he did,
following his Word,
which brings us nearer to you,
guiding us out of the darkness,
into your light.

Father, we understand that we know little,
even though the world has changed so much.
The mystery of life remains the same
and we still fear the unknown.

Comfort us
as we place our trust
in your healing love.

Amen.

44

SUSTAINABLE DEVELOPMENT GOALS: INDIGO

The United Nations Sustainable Development Goals for Indigo are:

- Peace
- Justice
- Strong institutions
- Partnerships for the goals

These goals work towards peaceful societies where all people have access to justice and basic freedoms. They aim to promote the rule of law and to reduce corruption so that all institutions are accountable to the people. Where corruption exists, states lose the money needed for vital resources. In developing nations, this money is the lifeline necessary to bring the population out of poverty. Strong institutions are needed to solve this problem.

The births of one in four children under five years old are not recorded and so they do not have a legal identity.

This makes it harder to access justice, social services and other forms of support.

In 2018, the United Nations recorded its highest number of people displaced by war, conflict and persecution, over 70 million. Without peace, very little progress can be made to solve ongoing problems.

Partnerships for the goals, acknowledges the fact that nothing can be achieved without cooperation, international investment and support for developing countries.

Innovative technology is needed to provide sustainable solutions. The United Nations seeks to work with all nations to make a significant difference to all people.

Prayer

Almighty Father,
we pray for all parts of the world
where there is violence,
war,
and hatred.

Please bring healing to those
whose damaged lives
have given rise to feelings of bitterness,
causing them to inflict pain and suffering
on the innocent.

We pray for all those who live in fear,
who are homeless,
and who mourn the loss
of loved ones.

Give them strength to face each day
and hope for a new dawn
of peace and healing.

Help those who seek peaceful coexistence
to find workable solutions,
so that a way through hatred and intolerance
can be found.

We pray for an end to corruption
and for access to justice
for all.

Amen.

PURPLE

45

NOBILITY

She makes herself coverings; her clothing is fine linen and purple.

Proverbs 31:22

Strength and dignity are her clothing, and she laughs at the time to come. She opens her mouth with wisdom, and the teaching of kindness is on her tongue.

31:25-26

reflection

Purple was and is a regal colour. Its use reflected the position of the wearer. Judges 8 tells us of the purple garments worn by the kings of Midian, showing their royalty.

Proverbs 31 refers to the clothing of a woman. She is certainly a noble and respected woman who receives praise and so the mention of purple cloth provides an important comment on her position. Purple dye was expensive to produce. A purple dye from the time of King David was found early in 2021 in Israel at a site in Timna, around 137 miles south of Jerusalem. The shade of purple was found in the body of molluscs and was said to be the most valued of dyes.

Prayer

Eternal Father,
we know that true nobility is found
in reaching out to others
in your name.

The richness of finery
is not everything.
The capable wife of Proverbs
was more precious than jewels
because of her wisdom
and her kindness.

May we all look beneath the surface
to find our true worth.
Through you,
and with the guidance of your Word,
may we find the nobility of service
and love.

Amen.

46

RICH MAN

> There was a rich man who was dressed in purple and fine linen and who feasted sumptuously every day.
> Luke 16:19

reflection

Jesus told the parable of the rich man and Lazarus. Once again, the colour purple is used to show how rich the man was. The rich man had a poor man at his gate called Lazarus, who was covered in sores. The parable suggests that the poor man did not receive any food from the rich man and was starving.

When both of the men died, Lazarus went to heaven to be with Abraham but the rich man was in hell being tormented. The rich man called out but was told that he could not get near to Lazarus.

The parable reminds us that we are not as important as

we think and that if we ignore the poor and those less fortunate than ourselves, we will be punished after death.

Christians are instructed to love their neighbour as themselves, according to the second greatest commandment and so they should not fall victim to this message if they follow the word of Christ.

When the man asks can anyone be sent to warn my brothers of this pitfall, he is told that he had Moses and the prophets to listen to and that was sufficient.

Prayer

Eternal Father,
please forgive us
when we fail
to do your will.

Sometimes we look
without seeing,
and it is convenient.

At other times
we intend to do something,
but it does not happen.

May we always be aware
of the difficulties of those around us
and willing to help.

Help us to act
on our good intentions.

And may we understand
that appearance is not everything
and earthly riches
do not store up riches
in Heaven.

Guide us to listen
and to heed your Word.

Help us to make our life journey
a time of learning.

Amen.

47

JESUS, KING OF THE JEWS

> And they clothed him in a purple cloak and after twisting some thorns into a crown, they put it on him. And they began saluting him,' Hail, King of the Jews!' They struck his head with a reed, spat upon him, and knelt down in homage to him. After mocking him, they stripped him of the purple cloak and put his own clothes on him. Then they led him out to crucify him.
>
> Mark 15:17-20.

reflection

The purple robe was to show that he was a king and this was a royal colour. Here, the reason was to mock and not to glorify and the robe was removed before Jesus was taken to be crucified. When he was brought before Pilate, Jesus was accused of claiming he was a king.

Mark 15:2 Pilate asked him, ‘ Are you the King of the Jews? He answered him,’ You say so.’

Jesus made no other reply to the charges and Pilate could not find any guilt in Jesus, but when he asked the crowd what he should do with the man they called ‘ King of the Jews’, they shouted ‘ Crucify him!’

The purple robe continues this theme. The King is being crucified and the people have changed from those who scattered palm leaves before Jesus crying out Hosanna, to a mob who had now turned against him. The description tells us so much more as Christians because to us, Jesus is our King. He is our earthly and heavenly king.

Prayer

Heavenly Father,
we give thanks for Jesus Christ,
ur saviour and king.

We worship him
and know that we will see him
in majesty with you
in Heaven.

Lord Jesus came to us on earth
to show us the way to you
and his heavenly kingdom.

Blessed are those
who glorify his holy name,
even though they have not seen him.

We hold strong to the faith
brought to us by the saviour.
Shouting loud hosannas,
we follow him to glory.

Amen.

48

KINGSHIP

> In the time of King Herod, after Jesus was born in Bethlehem of Judea, wise men from the East came to Jerusalem, asking, 'Where is the child who has been born king of the Jews? For we observed his star at its rising, and have come to pay him homage.
>
> Matthew 2: 1-2.

reflection

The wise men come from the east searching for the baby king. From his birth, Jesus is a king who is visited by kings bearing gifts of gold, frankincense and myrrh. The wise men were shown to be more clever than the wicked Herod, because they did not return to give him news of the special baby.

Jesus is the promised Messiah whose kingdom is in heaven. This is the reason for the heavenly sign of a star. The kings from a far off place remind us of the significance of this baby. The star of Bethlehem has remained an important symbol of Christ, who is the light of the world.

Prayer

Eternal Father,
we thank you for sending your son, Jesus
Christ,
to be our King.

The light of the Christ star leads us,
as the wise men were led to the child.

We worship him
in loud hosannas,
as the crowds did,
when he rode into Jerusalem.

May we be guided by his words
and healing love,
so that we may reach out to others
in his name.

Help us always to hold his example before us
and to glory in the empty cross
which showed that he had defeated
death itself: Alleluia!

Amen.

49

LYDIA

A certain woman named Lydia, a worshipper of God, was listening to us; she was from the city of Thyatira and a dealer in purple cloth. The Lord opened her heart to listen eagerly to what was said by Paul. Acts 16:14

reflection

In the Acts of the Apostles, we meet a lady called Lydia. She was a dealer in purple cloth and therefore a woman of some importance, who appeared to be independent. At this time when women were usually subject to men, this is a woman of substance who was involved in the trade of expensive goods. 'She and her household were baptized,' which means that she had influence and control over others in the household. She was an early convert to Christianity and someone who invited Paul, Silas and Timothy to stay at her home. The importance of a wealthy woman of influence as a convert can be imagined. She was able to bring others to Christianity by her power and example. Paul says that she received the word because she was chosen to witness for Lord Jesus.

Prayer

Heavenly Father,
we give thanks for all those
who have witnessed for your love.

For the early Christians,
the first to hear the special message
and to recognise the love of our saviour.
They led the way
in difficult and dangerous times
when it was not easy to be a Christian.

We pray for all Christians today
who suffer persecution
for their faith.
May they receive your blessing
and healing strength.
We hold them especially in our hearts
and prayers.

Amen.

50

NABOTH'S VINEYARD

> 'Have you found me, O my enemy?' He answered, 'I have found you. Because you have sold yourself to do what is evil in the sight of the Lord, I will bring disaster on you.'
>
> 1 Kings 21:20

reflection

Purple is the colour of grapes. Vines and vineyards certainly play a part in the Bible. 1 Kings 21 tells the story of Naboth's vineyard. It is a tale of jealousy and evil.

King Ahab of Samaria failed to persuade Naboth to relinquish his vineyard for money or a replacement. This refusal was not well received by King Ahab and Jezebel, his wife came up with an evil plan to obtain the vineyard which involved having Naboth executed on a false charge of cursing

God and the king. Naboth was stoned to death and Ahab went to take control of the vineyard.

The Lord spoke to Elijah and sent him to speak to Ahab. Jezebel was also to be fed to the dogs. When Ahab dressed in sackcloth, the Lord relented but said that he would bring disaster on Ahab's son's family.

This is a story of retribution and repentance, but vengeance was only delayed so that the sins of the father were to be borne by descendants. Today we would find this difficult to accept and would feel that if mercy could not be granted, Ahab and Jezebel should have paid the debt for the evil they committed.

Christianity brought a new covenant of love with the two greatest commandments and Jesus himself by his death to overcome sin, allowed us to be able to seek God's mercy through prayer.

Prayer

Heavenly Father,
please forgive us
when we have unworthy thoughts.

Help us to reject any feelings of resentment
or jealousy,
using reason and love
to drive away evil.

Help us to understand
that we can't always have
what we want.

May we see the good in others always
and seek to put things right
if they appear to be wrong.

May we be quick to forgive
and slow to judge
all people.
Help us to understand
that we always learn
from our relationships
with others.

Amen.

51

SUSTAINABLE DEVELOPMENT GOALS: PURPLE

The United Nations Sustainable Development Goals for Purple are:

- Decent Work
- Economic Growth

Sustainable economic growth is necessary to drive progress and this must be for all nations, so that there is a more equal world economy. Greater divisions have opened up between poorer and wealthier countries and this has been widened by the global pandemic.

Unemployment has and will grow because of the world health situation. Gender inequality worsens at these times and this has a detrimental impact on communities.People need work so that they can provide for themselves and their families. Work also gives a sense of well being and self respect.

GAYNOR COBB

Prayer

Heavenly Father,
we pray for our world,
for all nations.

Hold all those who are suffering ill health
in your loving arms.

We pray for healing for each country
as it recovers from the pandemic
and its consequences.

We pray for the bereaved,
the isolated,
and those without work.

We give thanks for the loving support
within communities,
where the hungry have been fed
and the lonely comforted.

May all governments work together
in cooperation
to move forward together.

Amen.

VIOLET

52

ADVENT

The people who walked in darkness have seen a great light; those who lived in a land of deep darkness – on them light has shined. You have multiplied the nation, you have increased its joy.
Isaiah 9:2-3

For a child has been born for us, a son given to us; authority rests upon his shoulders and he is named Wonderful Counsellor, Mighty God.
Isaiah 9:6-7

reflection

Violet is a liturgical colour for Advent symbolising preparation. When purple is combined with the blue of Mary's robe, the violet produced is a softer colour, appropriate for the Advent season. The church is preparing for the arrival of a special baby: the Christ child. This is a special time when we think of the power of light and are able to reach out to others in fellowship.

Isaiah predicts the coming of the Messiah. Jesus is the light of the world, who will lead people away from the deepest darkness. Christ will come to bring hope for the world. These are words familiar in Handel's Messiah. The colour purple/violet connects the baby to the arrival of a king. The spiritual kingdom of Christ is described here with his growing authority and the upholding of eternal justice and peace.

Prayer

Eternal Father,
We give thanks
for the coming of Jesus Christ
to be our saviour.

The world had waited for Emmanuel,
to show the way
to you.

In the Advent season,
we prepare to celebrate his birth
once again.

The Prince of Peace,
bringing hope of salvation
to the world,
is found to be here with us.

The gift of the Christ child
showed your love
for us all.

Help us to love him
in return.
We pray that his authority grows indeed,
that all people are drawn
to hear the good news
of life eternal.

Amen.

53

LENT

Again, the devil took him to a very high mountain and showed him all the kingdoms of the world and their splendour; and he said to him, 'All these I will give you, if you will fall down and worship me.' Jesus said to him, 'Away with you, Satan! for it is written, "Worship the Lord your God, and serve only him."' Then the devil left him, and suddenly angels came and waited on him.

Matthew 4:8-11

reflection

Violet is a liturgical colour for Lent, symbolising sacrifice and the emotional and physical suffering of Jesus before and during the passion. It is during this time that we remind ourselves what it means to be a Christian. We prepare as Jesus did to renew our faith and to celebrate the greatest Christian festival of Eastertide.

Jesus himself withdrew into the wilderness to fast and meditate. He fasted for forty days and nights. Satan tempted him with food and thoughts of proving his divinity. Jesus was strong, confirming that man lives according to the word of God and does not put God to the test. Jesus prepared his body for suffering in a particular way, gaining control over the physical and testing his mental strength.

How often do people on earth believe that behaving in the wrong way gives them success? We pray to be spared temptation and yet it takes so many forms. Jesus faced the greatest temptation and the difficulty of knowing that death approached and how it would happen. We have different challenges but Lent is an opportunity to think about how we are living and how we come to God.

Prayer

Eternal Father,
help us to examine our lives
during Lent,
so that we may prepare to celebrate
the resurrection
of Lord Jesus.

We can only walk the way of the Lord
in Holy Week,
if we have searched
our own souls.

May we see Lent
as a time for thought
rather than mere denial.

We pray that we will rededicate our lives
to you,
as Jesus himself did
when he overcame
the tempter.

Help us to discover the way forward,
in your transforming love.

Amen.

54

THE TEMPLE OF SOLOMON

> Beaten silver is brought from Tarshish, and gold from Uphaz. They are the work of the artisan and of the hands of the goldsmith; their clothing is blue and purple; they are all the product of skilled workers. But the Lord is the true God; He is the living God and the everlasting King. At his wrath the earth quakes, and the nations cannot endure his indignation.
>
> Jeremiah 10:9-10

reflection

2 Chronicles describes the building of the temple of Solomon which was the First Temple, built in Jerusalem and completed in 957 BC. The temple was built for the Lord God and did not have idols within it.

Jeremiah 10 tells us that the Lord is the true God but

that idols had been made with clothing of blue and purple. Although the idols were beautiful, it was stupid to make them and they put the craftsman to shame. The people had slipped back into the worship of idols in the way that many people have today.

Prayer

Eternal Father,
you are indeed the Living God.
You have filled us
with your Holy Spirit.

When you sent your son, Jesus Christ,
to fill us with the living water of eternal life,
you showed us how to reach out
in your name.

Help us to reject
the idols of modern life.
May we serve you in completeness.

Lead us towards
a deeper understanding
of everything around us,
seen and unseen.

Amen.

55

PRIESTLY VESTMENTS

> They shall make the ephod of gold, of blue, purple and crimson yarns, and of fine twisted linen, skilfully worked. It shall have two shoulder-pieces attached to its two edges, so that it may be joined together. The decorated band on it shall be of the same workmanship and materials, of gold, of blue, purple , and crimson yarns, and of fine twisted linen.
>
> Exodus 28: 6-8

reflection

Exodus 28 describes the priestly vestments for Moses' brother Aaron and his sons that were to be made under the instruction of the Lord.

Aaron's vestments were sacred and very beautiful. These vestments were for the priests to serve in the tabernacle which contained the Ark of the Covenant. The ephod which was a garment to be worn over the robes, was especially decorative and of value. The breastplate was to be made in the style of the ephod but decorated with precious and semi-precious stones.

God gave instructions so that the vestments would be just as he desired. This tells us how important they were. It also gives directions to help worship today. The clergy wear special clothes for a reason and these are all a part of our preparation for worship. It matters how we approach our worship and the sacraments.

Prayer

Heavenly Father,
we praise you for your glory.

May we care
for our special places
of worship.

Although we know
that you are with us everywhere,
it is right that we have somewhere sacred
to find you.

Our worship leaders dress to show reverence
to you.
Their clothes reflect the church year
with times to think about.
We are reminded of your Word
by robes and altar hangings.

They show our sense of wonder
as we come before you,
in humility and awe.

Outside,
in your creation,
nature's beauty
serves to celebrate your majesty.

Alleluia!

56

AMETHYST

> You shall set in it four rows of stones. A row of carnelian, chrysolite, and emerald shall be the first row; and the second row a turquoise, a sapphire, and a moonstone; and the third row a jacinth, an agate, and an amethyst; and the fourth row a beryl, an onyx, and a jasper; they shall be set in gold filigree.
> Exodus 28:17-20

reflection

The instructions given were very precise and the vestments would show how special the tabernacle was. This made it clear to the Israelites that worship was important and that the living God expected to be venerated in glory even though he did not wish to be worshipped with idols. The amethyst mentioned was included for piety, calm and for forgiveness.

The violet colour of amethyst produces a feeling of calm, peacefulness and is regarded as spiritual.

Prayer

Eternal Father,
we worship you and glorify your holy name.
May we remember the importance
of setting aside time
for worship.

Sometimes we pray to you
asking for ourselves
and others.

May we remember to give thanks
and to praise you
with joyfulness.

We know that we can reach out to you
anywhere
and we glory in your wonderful creation
all around us.

Father,
help us to value and care
for the places we visit
for worship.

We know it is important
o preserve places

devoted to you,
and to your son, our saviour,
Jesus Christ.

May they always hold a special place
in our hearts,
there to meet you,
in the quiet of your house.

Amen.

57

TO DREAM

> In the last days it will be, God declares, that I will pour out my Spirit upon all flesh, and your sons and daughters shall prophesy, and your young men shall see visions, and your old men shall dream dreams.
>
> Acts 2:17

reflection

The violet amethyst stone is called achlama in Hebrew, which is like the word halam meaning dream. In St. John's dream described in Revelation, the foundations of the walls of the holy city of Jerusalem were covered in jewels, with the twelfth being amethyst.

There are many accounts of dreams of prophecy in the Bible, including Joseph's and Daniel's dreams. In the verse from Acts, God promises dreams, visions and prophecy at the end of the world.

Prayer

Eternal Father,
we give thanks for quiet times
of calm contemplation.

Help us to find the time
to come to you.

May we think and pray
for our brothers and sisters
in difficulties
across the world.

Jesus gave us his peace
to share with others.
As Christian disciples help us to show
his calming love.

We pray for times to reach you,
for forgiveness,
and for quiet inner strength,
so that we may continue on our journey
of healing faith.

Amen.

58

SUSTAINABLE DEVELOPMENT GOALS: VIOLET

The United Nations Sustainable Development Goals for violet are:

- Reduced inequalities

This goal deals with inequalities within countries themselves and also among nations. It matters because poor, developing countries have more inequalities and these cause suffering which is difficult to eradicate. Health, education and employment suffer because of social inequality often based on race, gender or religion.

We need to work to wipe out all inequalities so that all people have opportunities to thrive and everyone is treated with the same level of justice, freedom, respect and dignity. In many ways this goal links with all other goals because we should offer everyone a fair and decent way of life.

Prayer

Heavenly Father,
We pray for our world at this time
when there are so many problems.

May we work tirelessly
to achieve equality
for all people.

Help us to hold strong standards
of freedom, justice,
and opportunity.

We pray for equality of race, gender,
and religion throughout the world,
allowing all people to access education,
food and housing.

We pray that your love will reach everyone,
but pray especially for the poor
and the disadvantaged.

May they be part of a better future,
steadfast in the love of Jesus Christ,
our saviour.

Amen.

WHITE

59

ENJOY LIFE

> Go, eat your bread with enjoyment, and drink your wine with a merry heart; for God has long ago approved what you do. Let your garments always be white; do not let oil be lacking on your head.
>
> Ecclesiastes 9:7-8

reflection

The message here is to enjoy life and live with a merry heart. If we have gratitude and we are able to make the most of every day and live it to the full, we will have done as much as is possible. It is still possible to serve God and to be a Christian if we are enjoying life.

Christians are often happiest when their lives are fulfilled by serving others. Our white garments remind us of more serious responsibilities and the oil anoints us with the love of God. Even when we are relaxed and enjoying life, we are aware of our higher spiritual responsibilities. The chapter goes on to talk about wisdom and folly, suggesting that in truth, we must never forget our purpose.

Prayer

Heavenly Father,
we give thanks for the joy of life,
for friendship, warmth and love.

Help us to live each day to the full,
reaching out to those we meet
with smiles and a helping hand.

Walking life's path,
burdens are lighter
if we share them.

May the love of Christ
inspire our hearts
to bring his light into the world.

Holding high the cross,
may our wisdom remain,
so that we never forget
the higher purpose of justice,
equality and love,
for all.

Amen.

60

CLEANSING AND PARDON

Have mercy on me, O God, according to your steadfast love; according to your abundant mercy blot out my transgressions. Wash me thoroughly from my iniquity, and cleanse me from my sin.

Psalm 51: 1-2

You desire truth in the inward being, therefore teach me wisdom in my secret heart. Purge me with hyssop, and I shall be clean; wash me, and I shall be whiter than snow.

Psalm 51: 6-7

reflection

Psalm 51 is a psalm of David for cleansing and pardon. David is in need of God's forgiveness, compassion and mercy. He knows that it is only through God that he can find the way forward after sin. When we disappoint God, when we are sinful, we depend on God's mercy. He can make us whole again if we are contrite. Only God can make us whiter than snow. Each time, we go out into the world to try again.

Prayer

Eternal Father,
please forgive my sins,
which are many.

Father God,
you are merciful and I give you thanks
for your compassion.

You understand when I do wrong.
Cleanse me so that I may restore my soul.
Fill me with your Holy Spirit,
so that I may try once again
be as you would wish.

Help me to pick myself up
when I have failed you.
Only you can make me
whiter than snow.
I do not presume
to think of myself as so clean,
except through your mercy.

Amen.

61

THE ANCIENT ONE

> As I watched, thrones were set in place, and an Ancient One took his throne; his clothing was white as snow, and the hair of his head like pure wool; his throne was fiery flames, and its wheels were burning fire. Daniel 7:9

reflection

The book of Daniel tells us of Daniel's dreams and visions. The Ancient One is a mysterious figure who is worshipped because he is on a throne. Daniel 7:10 tells us he was served by a thousand thousand and attended by ten thousand times ten thousand. Is this God the Father? With the numbers of those in attendance, it would seem to be so. Daniel's visions tell us a great deal about heaven and the perception of the afterlife.

Prayer

Eternal Father,
we do not know the mysteries
of heaven and the universe.

Help us to keep an open mind
about all things.

May we learn not to judge quickly
with prejudicial thoughts.

We give thanks
for the wisdom of your Word,
guiding us forward.

Help us to grow
in the understanding of our faith,
through the experience
of our years.

Amen.

62

PROPHECY ABOUT JESUS

> As I watched in the night visions, I saw one like a human being coming with the clouds of Heaven. And he came to the Ancient One and was presented before him. To him was given dominion and glory and kingship, that all peoples, nations, and languages should serve him. His dominion is an everlasting dominion that shall not pass away, and his kingship is one that shall never be destroyed.
>
> Daniel 7:13-14

reflection

Once again, the Old Testament has foretold the coming of Jesus to reign as king for eternal life. He rules over all nations of heaven and earth.

Jesus was presented before the Ancient One. Is this Jesus presented to the Almighty Father?

The passage reminds us of Isaiah, when the prophecy is given about the coming of Jesus, so loved during the Advent season.

Daniel's dream is reminiscent of The Revelation of John. The description of the Ancient One with hair like pure wool, is similar to the figure like the Son of Man at the beginning of the vision.

Prayer

Eternal Father,
we may not be able to speak
all the languages
of the world,
enabling us to spread the good news
of our saviour.
We may not always understand others,
even when they speak as we do.

Help us to be open to your Word
and to the needs of your children.
May we offer a listening ear
but not a judging heart.

Let us hear the cries of the poor
and underprivileged
and respond with Christian charity.
Through your Holy Spirit,
may we seek to show your love.

Amen.

63

ANGELS AT THE TOMB

> But Mary stood weeping outside the tomb. As she wept, she bent over to look into the tomb; and she saw two angels in white, sitting where the body of Jesus had been lying, one at the head and the other at the feet. They said to her, 'Woman, why are you weeping?' She said to them, ' They have taken away my Lord, and I do know where they have laid him.' When she had said this, she turned round and saw Jesus standing there, but she did not know that it was Jesus. John 20:11-14

reflection

The angels in white show peacefulness after the violence of the crucifixion. They are an indication that everything has changed. The body has gone and they are sitting where Jesus had been laid to rest. Mary speaks to them as though all this was normal, thinking that the body had been taken away. Her reaction makes sense to us, even though we can see that something amazing has happened. In the shock of the situation, it is not easy to think clearly.

The presence of angels at the tomb and of Jesus in the garden, suggest that they had been around the Saviour. Angels are God's messengers and they may have brought messages to him as well as to Mary Magdalene.

Easter Day gives us the celebration because we know the end of this part of the story. We can say Alleluia!

Prayer

Almighty Father,
Alleluia! Alleluia!
We give thanks
for the great message,
the good news from your angels,
that the Lord is risen!

Help us to look for your messages,
to receive your Word.

Jesus walked among us
to bring us close to you.
On our own road to Emmaus,
may we recognise him.

Amen

64

THE ASCENSION

When he had said this, as they were watching, he was lifted up, and a cloud took him out of their sight. While he was going and they were gazing up towards heaven, suddenly two men in white robes stood by them. They said, 'Men of Galilee, why do you stand looking up towards heaven? This Jesus, who has been taken up from you into heaven, will come in the same way as you saw him go into heaven.'

Acts 1: 9-11

reflection

The Ascension of Jesus to heaven is described in the Acts of the Apostles. Jesus told his disciples that they would receive the Holy Spirit and that they would continue his work. They were bewildered by what they had seen and it must have been difficult to think about the uncertain future. They had to find the courage that they feared would never come to them, but with the Holy Spirit, God showed them the way forward as he does with all of us if we place our faith in him.

Again, two angels are there as messengers to explain what has happened to the disciples. The explanation is also given to help the word of the Bible. Angels are almost like special narrators because they tell us important details that could not be known to the onlookers, who are often the disciples, as in this case.

Prayer

Eternal Father,
we look towards Heaven,
yet we are not able to see Jesus.
Our vision of him
is in our hearts.
Deepen our faith in him.

We know that we are blessed
because we believe,
even though we have not seen,
as Thomas had.

Help us to receive your Word
through the saviour.
Guide our understanding
and our desire
to follow where he leads us.

We know that one day
we will be with him,
if we seek eternal life.

Fill us with the power of your Holy Spirit
to find him in prayer.

Amen.

65

SUSTAINABLE DEVELOPMENT GOALS: WHITE

The United Nations Sustainable Development Goal for White is:

- World peace

World peace is such an important goal because, without peace, nothing can be achieved, and we know that war and conflict lead to displaced people, poverty, hunger and lack of every opportunity including education.

Prayer

Heavenly Father,
we pray for all people
who suffer because of conflict.

We think of child soldiers,
vulnerable young lives

shattered by war.
May they find protection
and a way back to their communities.

We pray for healing and understanding
in these difficult situations.
May there be a way forward.

We pray for people
in places of destruction.
May they rebuild
from the rubble and dust.

We pray for the seeds of hope
to take root once again.
May the displaced
find a welcome
in a new area,
or an opportunity
to return home.

Father,
we are so in need
of your healing love
to share.

Amen.

SILVER

66

PIECES OF SILVER

> Then one of the twelve, who was called Judas Iscariot, went to the chief priests and said, ' What will you give me if I betray him to you?' They paid him thirty pieces of silver. And from that moment he began to look for an opportunity to betray him.
>
> Matthew 26:14-16

reflection

We find the most infamous pieces of silver in history in Matthew 26, which tells of the plot to kill Jesus by the chief priests and elders. We do not know why Judas betrayed Jesus but we suspect that it was meant to be in order to accomplish the mission of the saviour.

Judas took money and yet it seems unimportant that he had the silver coins. They were of value and yet they only brought him death. We wonder if Judas expected Jesus to be a leader who would overcome the Romans and free the Jews. Jesus was the Messiah and Judas had seen the miracles he had performed during his ministry.

When Jesus entered Jerusalem on a humble donkey, Judas gradually began to realise that he was not going to be a revolutionary king. The kingdom of Jesus was of another world and a different kind. Jesus knew of the plot by Judas and that his disciples would also panic and desert him.

Prayer

Eternal Father,

we ask that our souls are refined and purified in your service.

May we find a way through the trials of life on earth,
learning as we walk the many paths.
Help us to search for those who suffer as we do.
In fellowship within your church, we reach out,
even when the way ahead is not clear.
May we seek you in prayer, alone and together.
Help us to understand, even if we still lack the wisdom of your truth.

Amen.

67

WORDS OF THE LORD

> Then Jesus said to them, ' You will all become deserters because of me this night; for it is written, 'I will strike the shepherd, and the sheep of the flock will be scattered.' But after I am raised up, I will go ahead of you to Galilee.'
>
> Matthew 26: 31-32

reflection

Once again, Jesus talked of being the good shepherd and this time it was the disciples who were the sheep. All had been written and prophesied. He told them that he would see them in Galilee and this should have been at the heart of their faith after his death. The Bible does not make it clear that the disciples held on to these words of Jesus but it would seem likely that they would have thought back over his words, especially those spoken in the last days in Jerusalem.

Jesus told them that their sorrow would turn to joy and that their hearts would rejoice when they saw him. The disciples found it difficult to understand what Jesus meant and yet there were so many words to think back to when the time came. Later, Jesus gave his disciples hope for the future. He had conquered everything and so would they. They would receive the means to do this through the Holy Spirit.

Prayer

Loving Father,
we give thanks for Jesus, our good shepherd.
We are his sheep,
wandering through this world.
Sometimes lost,
we seek him to guide us safely home.
Even the disciples scattered
at the critical time.
Somehow this comforts us
because we know that they feared
as we often do.
Filled with the Holy Spirit,
their sorrow turned to joy.
May we also receive the peace
brought by the saviour.
In his conquering love,
may we do your will.

Amen.

68

THE LOST COIN

'Or what woman having ten silver coins, if she loses one of them, does not light a lamp, sweep the house, and search carefully until she finds it? When she has found it, she calls together her friends and neighbours, saying, 'Rejoice with me, for I have found the coin that I had lost.' Just so, I tell you, there is joy in the presence of the angels of God over one sinner who repents.'

Luke 15:8-10

reflection

We are delighted to think of heaven's happiness at our repentance when we sin. This is the hope given by Jesus that God is merciful and when we fall down, we can still get up again and carry on. There is a beautiful story about a conveyor belt with perfect vases on it. Some fall onto the ground and are chipped, cracked or broken. These are the ones that Jesus wants.

We are told that Jesus spent his time with tax collectors and sinners. The perfect ones do not need him, but the imperfect sinners do. We are assured of forgiveness and the opportunity to be our better selves.

Prayer

Eternal Father,
we thank you for your understanding.
So often we fall short
of perfection.

Our sins trouble us as they should
and we turn to you
in repentance.

In your compassion,
you grant us grace
and renewal.

We return to daily life
and try yet again.

We give thanks
for Heaven's rejoicing
and for your eternal love
and mercy.

Amen.

69

WISE WORDS

> A word fitly spoken is like apples of gold in a setting of silver.
>
> Proverbs 25:11

reflection

This is a reminder of the importance of wisdom. It is necessary to think carefully about the words we speak because they are valuable. The right word at the right time can make a huge difference and we are warned to think before we speak.

Later, Proverbs warns that one who bears false witness against a neighbour is like a sword or sharp arrow. Here, the warning is about the damage of words. Where lies are told, words are like a weapon of war. Use words wisely and do not lie, especially about other people.

Words are either precious metals of beauty when used for good purposes, or sharp weapons that can abuse others.

Prayer

Heavenly Father,
We give thanks for the guidance
of your Word.

May we take it to our hearts
and allow our minds
to dwell on it.

Help us to think about the words
we speak.
May we consider how
and what
we say.

Help us to weigh our thoughts
and words carefully,
so that we help rather than hurt others.

May we put safely away our sharp tongues,
as we would a harmful sword.

Help us to find words of love and beauty
more like apples of gold,
set in silver.

Amen.

70

REFINED AND TESTED

> For you, O God, have tested us; you have tried us as silver is tried. You brought us into the net; you laid burdens on our backs; you let people ride over our heads; we went through fire and water; yet you have brought us out to a spacious place.
>
> Psalm 66: 10-12

reflection

The psalms give examples of the way God tests our lives and souls. We think of the way the beautiful metal is made and refined because we are created by God. We are always changing but our challenge is to ensure that we change for the better.

Life is full of problems to solve so that our souls become the best that they can be. After the struggles and trials, we are brought to heaven, to a place of beauty. We have changed ourselves and have become beautiful, like silver. This is our reward.

Psalm 12:6 explains that after our difficulties, we can be sure of God's help because his promises are like silver which is refined seven times over.

Prayer

Eternal Father,
we pray for strength when we are tested.
We know that our souls grow
in the depth of your love.

Help us to be ready
for the challenge of life,
knowing that we are only given
what we can bear.

Your promises, like silver,
inspire us to greater goodness.

We hold before us
the example of your son,
our saviour, Jesus Christ.

May we strive to be like him,
reaching out to others in your name,
so that we too may find the way
to Heaven.

Amen.

71

THE BEAUTY OF GOD'S LOVE

And I will put this third into the fire, refine them as one refines silver, and test them as gold is tested. They will call on my name, and I will answer them. I will say, ' They are my people', and they will say, 'The Lord is our God.'

Zechariah 13:9

reflection

Once again we are told about the testing of the precious metals of silver and gold. The value and beauty of these makes the point that when we are refined and improved, we are worthy of God and we have something to aspire to. We have been refined in the fire and have come through the test, like gold set in silver, at last we have arrived in the beauty of God's truth and love.

Prayer

Eternal Father,
we give you thanks
for the beauty of your creation,
of which we are part.

We are indeed refined and improved,
yet, as people of the earth,
we ask your forgiveness.

So often,
we disagree with each other.
Person against person,
community against community,
nation against nation,
we argue.

We pray for peace and reconciliation.
May we reach out to one another,
whoever and wherever we are,
in healing love,
to share your peace.

Amen.

72

SUSTAINABLE DEVELOPMENT GOALS: SILVER AND GOLD

The United Nations Sustainable Development Goal for Silver and Gold is:

- Responsible consumption and production

This means living within our means as a world. Using resources sensibly, so that we have enough for everyone is most important for the future. We must be able to renew and replace the things we use, so that production can be sustained. We are developing a greener economy in many ways but we must all contribute to this effort.

Prayer

Heavenly Father,
we pray for the future of the world.
We have used resources without thinking
and now we face the hardship of reality.

We know that we cannot sustain this lifestyle
which leads to destruction
in so many ways.

Help us to think of our beautiful planet
and to care for your creation,
so that generations to come
can flourish as we have.

We pray that populations
may be controlled
so that all can have food.

May we uphold equality,
So that all people
may share in a brighter, caring future,
full of opportunity.

Amen.

73

THE GOAL AT THE END OF THE RAINBOW

> For you shall go out in joy, and be led back in peace, the mountains and the hills before yourself shall burst into song, and all the trees of the field shall clap their hands. Instead of the thorn shall come up the cypress; instead of the brier shall come up the myrtle; and it shall be to the Lord for a memorial, for an everlasting sign that shall not be cut off.
>
> Isaiah 55:12

reflection

As we go forward with an optimistic rainbow-like outlook, we look to the Bible for a sense of joy. The rainbow is a covenant with God. The prophecy speaks of a special chosen one who will bring freedom and justice.

We began with the rainbow and a covenant with God.

Christians believe that Jesus is the new covenant through his death to redeem sins and to bring us back to God's grace.

Jesus is an advocate in heaven because he understands our human frailty. Christ with life eternal dwells within us so that we are able to serve God in the power of the Holy Spirit. We are the 'living sacrifice' that Christ himself was when he died for us.

The power of this fellowship, given to us by Jesus through his disciples at the Last Supper, is not only of him but a sacred rite of dedication and renewal. In this way, Christians are helped to live their faith.

Prayer

Eternal Father,
we give thanks
for the power of Christ
within us.

He is our new covenant
with you.
With the power of the Holy Spirit,
we have life eternal.

Coming to your table,
the sacrament renews us
with a living faith.

Going out into the world,
we share your love
with others.

The message of salvation
through the cross of Jesus
empowers us.

We are strong
in his love
and his peace.

We pray for a powerful presence
of Christ
walking with us.

Amen.

And so to the future . . .

74

UNITED NATIONS SUSTAINABLE DEVELOPMENT GOALS

If the global population reaches 9.6 billion by 2050 as expected, we could only sustain our present way of living by increasing natural resources. It would require the equivalent of almost three planets to do this. This is a very serious problem but many people in the world have the will to make a difference.

Science has given us the way forward to make sensible decisions but this does mean making positive changes. We have to find the end of the rainbow for ourselves as a global society.

The seventeen United Nations Sustainable Development Goals are a worldwide commitment, not only for the aim of making our planet a better place but of saving it for future generations. It is focused on a plan of achievement by 2030, although it is likely to extend beyond that time. How much progress we make towards completion depends on our own determination. As church communities, I hope that we will hold these goals in our prayers and work locally, nationally and internationally for their success. I have faith that this will be our promise.

During the global pandemic of 2020, many countries recorded a song of blessing. It was written by Chris Brown, Cody Carnes, Kari Jobe, and Steven Furtick, and was recorded into a large number of versions around the world. This beautiful blessing had a special significance at a difficult time.

Like the rainbow, it became a sign of hope, unity and God's love. It begins with the passage from Numbers 6:24-26, when the Lord gave the words of the blessing to Moses for the priests to bless the Israelites.

'The Lord bless you and keep you,
Make his face shine upon you
and be gracious to you.
The Lord turn his face toward you
and give you peace.'

The Goals

- No Poverty
- Zero Hunger
- Good Health and Well-Being
- Quality Education
- Gender Equality
- Clean Water and Sanitation
- Affordable and Clean Energy
- Decent Work and Economic Growth
- Industry, Innovation and Infrastructure
- Reduced Inequalities

- Sustainable Cities and Communities
- Responsible Consumption and Production
- Climate Action
- Life Below Water
- Life on Land
- Peace, Justice,and Strong Institutions
- Partnerships For The Goals

WHERE RAINBOWS MEET

Where Rainbows Meet is a community based organisation in the Vrygrond Township in Cape Town, South Africa. They deal with many problems within the area arising from poverty.

Working with vulnerable and disadvantaged groups, WRM provides a number of programmes offering support, including, human rights and legal advice, computer literacy and small business development.

The international development project helps women to gain confidence and gives support with social issues.

Their social support with domestic problems and substance abuse is of particular benefit in the township and they are trying to raise funds to open a women's refuge to support vulnerable families.

I visited the project and was impressed with their energy and commitment to supporting the community.

They certainly offer the hope shown in a rainbow and it is true to say that perhaps the rainbows do meet after all!

Their website is: www.whererainbowsmeet.org